UL[illegible]UTS: 7 [illegible] TO BURN FAT FAST AS HELL

By Brandon Carter

www.BrandonCarter.com

Disclaimer & Copyright

This book is not intended as a substitute for the medical advice of physicians. The reader should regularly consult a physician in matters relating to his/her health and particularly with respect to any symptoms that may require diagnosis or medical attention.

The information provided in this book is designed to provide helpful information on the subjects discussed. This book is not meant to be used, nor should it be used, to diagnose or treat any medical condition. For diagnosis or treatment of any medical problem, consult your own physician. The publisher and author are not responsible for any specific health or allergy needs that may require medical supervision and are not liable for any damages or negative consequences from any treatment, action, application or preparation, to any person reading or following the information in this book. References are provided for informational purposes only and do not constitute endorsement of any websites or other sources. Readers should be aware that the websites listed in this book may change.

Bro Laboratories
480 6th Avenue #219
New York, NY 10011
www.BroLaboratories.com

Table Of Contents

About The Author

My Name is Brandon Carter. I have been Personal trainer for over 10 years at some of the top gyms in New York City. I have worked as a fitness model for Nike, Adidas, Puma, Brand Jordan and more. I have also trained many professional athletes and fitness models.

My goal is to help as many people as possible reach their fitness goals. My blog (http://www.BrandonCarter.com) has helped hundreds of people do just that. Here are a few testimonials:

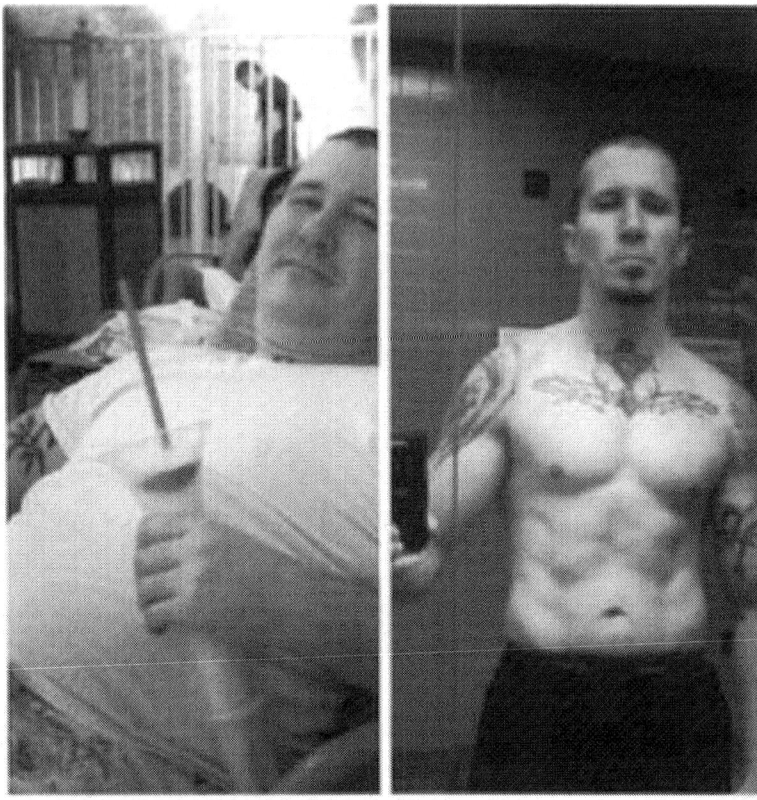

(Some people questioned the authenticity of this pic when I first posted it because his tattoo is on the other arm in the second pic. It is because he took the pic in the mirror. I don't want to get into the "science" of that, but if I take a pic of my reflection, my tattoos switch sides too. Like magic!)

"All of my coworkers, family and friends ask me how I lost all my weight (currently at a loss of 58 lbs) and built all of my muscle. I tell them that I used all that I learned from you as a base of my eating habits and workout plans. I wanted to thank you for all the helpful information and I wanted to send you a before and current (2 months ago) picture of myself so you can see my progress thanks to you. The before picture was a little over 1 year from the more current picture. I hope Brandon himself gets to see this because I would like him to know the huge impact his words and videos have had on my life and hopefully many others."

- Michael Alexand

"I watched your youtube videos, which helped me with my body transformation. Check out my weight loss album!"
- Kamari

"Results don't just come over night, and supplements can only do so much... But these workouts Brandon provides are the real deal! For real results and real motivation quit doing the same workouts and try something new! I did, and I'm seeing satisfying results already!!"
- Joshua Everett

"I'd like to thank you for everything you've done up til now. Thanks to you I was able to accomplish my FItness Goals in the past year. Here are 2 pics. Sorry for the before pic found no better one.Would be glad to see it on your Facebook site or homepage so that I can also motivate others to not give up best regards!"
- Christopher Scharner

"Hi Brandon, my name is Ergin YALI and I'm currently 17 years old. First of all I want to thank you for all the great and helpful information that I learnt from you and from your site. Most fitness instructors, and nutritionists I have talked at the past made me keep wasting my time and money, but you man, you are completely different. I learned almost all my eating and workout plans/tips from you.

Thanks again for sharing all your knowledge with me and others. Till 9 months ago I was 105 kg, now I m currently 70 kg. My waist reduced 143cm to 86 cm. No other words needed, photos describe my situation. I got leaner and also added a lot of muscle. I hope you get this mail man, because I would like you to know your words, tips, inspirational quotes and videos changed my life. I hope others can reach their goals too. Also you're a brilliant musician man, KEEP IT UP!!! (sorry for wrong sentences man, my english is not that great)."

- Ergin Yali

"I've 'worked out' for years...since before high school I was very active and played sports both in and outside of school. I was always climbing things and doing pushups & pullups wherever I could. In high school I started wrestling and weight training more consistently. Regardless of all my activity I never really achieved the body I wanted. I ate healthier than average and my activity was well above average including some of the toughest workouts you can imagine. This still wasn't good enough. It wasn't until I met Brandon and he taught me about things like proper supplementation, timing your workouts right in relation to your eating, and how to keep track of and measure my progress that I really started noticing results that I was happy with. His methods are simple and proven. Anyone can do it as long as they put the effort in. As always, Thanks B!"
- Brian Ryder

Apparently I inspire people not only to get in shape, but to get tattoos as well. You can see more testimonials on my blog: http://www.BrandonCarter.com

I believe you can achieve results like the ones above and even better! I am living proof that these 7 secrets work for anyone who applies them. I've learned through experimentation and application that these are the best and fastest proven ways to achieve your best body. It would be selfish to keep these secrets to myself so I'm sharing them all in this book. I hope they change your life like they have changed mine. Lets get to work!

Brandon Carter

Fitness Blog http://www.BrandonCarter.com
YouTube http://www.youtube.com/HighLifeWorkout
Facebook https://www.facebook.com/BigBrandonCarter
Twitter https://twitter.com/BCarterMusic
Instagram http://instagram.com/bcartermusic
SnapChat: @KillerCarter187

Introduction

"We are what we repeatedly do. Excellence, then, is not an act, but a habit."
-Aristotle

This book is a collection of some of the best methods I know to burn body fat in the least amount of time possible. I have been a personal trainer for over 10 years. I have worked for many of the top gyms in New York City. I have trained professional athletes and top models. I have also worked as a fitness model for Nike, Adidas, Jordan, Puma, and others. I say all that to say this: I know what I am talking about.

I have used every technique written here on myself and my clients over the years. They all work! You do NOT have to use them all at once. You can pick and choose what works according to your lifestyle. But the FASTEST way to get ripped would be to use ALL of the techniques at once. If you follow the outline for three months you will become more lean than you have ever been in your entire life!

In chapter one I will start with the most basic and easy fat burning method that I know of.. Each following chapter will be more advanced. I have seen MANY people get ripped with the info in chapter one alone! You can go as far down the rabbit hole as you would like.

WARNING: READ THIS BEFORE YOU GO ANY FURTHER!

In an effort to keep this book short, I have links to videos and blog posts that explain some of the topics in greater detail. Be sure to click on them if you need more clarity on a topic or if you want to see my video making skills.

I use foul language when I talk. I find it odd that someone would buy a book with the word "Hell" in the title then complain about any foul language. I deliberately put that word in the title to discourage more conservative people from buying it, KNOWING they would end up focusing on the wrong details. "Never criticize, condemn, or complain" said Dale Carnegie in his best selling self-help book, *How To Win Friends And Influence People.* Having that said, read that book first if you haven't yet done so, and ***if foul language offends you, please do not watch the videos. Thank you.***

To View The Bar Code Boxes, Download A "QR Code Scanner" On Your Smartphone To Scan And View The Links In The Following Pages... Enjoy!

SECRET #1: How To Burn Fat Without Counting Calories

"It's not the daily increase but daily decrease. Hack away at the unessential."
-Bruce Lee

In order to lose weight, you have to burn more calories than you take in. It's really that simple. But I know you are not going to count every calorie that you take in. Look, I have been training people for over a decade, and I know for a FACT that you are not going to count your calories. I could not even get the pro athletes and models that I have trained to do it! The ONLY people that I've ever seen do it right were competitive bodybuilders.

People often ask me "How many calories do you eat everyday?". The truth is that I NEVER count calories at all! I use a different system for tracking my food intake. I use the "Portion Size Method". In the video below I explain how the "Portion Size Method" works.

http://bit.ly/1ZRGJxW

Forget about counting calories! You do not need to count calories unless you are going to be on stage in a bodybuilding competition. For everyone else, I think that counting calories is too difficult and not sustainable. Some of you may be thinking "Hey, but I have this cool app on my phone that takes a pic of my food and counts the calories for me". I hate to be the bearer of bad news, but your app is full of shit and needless to say will be far from accurate. Your app is just guessing because it has no idea how the food was prepared, what kind of oil it was cooked in, or what ingredients are in the sauce.

That is my problem with counting calories, it's hard to be accurate. For example, my buddy just opened a restaurant here in New York. I help him out on the weekends; managing, hosting, and sometimes cooking too. If you came into our restaurant trying to count calories you would be shit out of luck because you would not know every ingredient that I put in the mashed potatoes, how much butter is in my special sauce, what kind of oil I used on the meat, etc... SOMETIMES I DON'T EVEN KNOW!!! Just kidding.

So if you want to count calories accurately you can forget about eating out. That means you cannot eat out with your friends and family or grab a bite to eat during your lunch break. ***The ONLY way to accurately count calories is to do what the pro bodybuilders and fitness competitors do - prepare ALL of their food at home, and take it with them in a cooler***. This way they can actually WEIGH their food on a scale and know EVERY ingredient in each meal so they are not guessing.

THIS is the ONLY way to accurately count your calories

If you are not prepping ALL of your food at home and taking it with you in a cooler, then you are not accurately counting calories. I don't know about you, but that seems like a lot of work. I KNOW it is effective (it is the MOST effective way to diet!), but I also know that I am not going to be able to sustain a lifestyle that requires me to eat all my food out of some goddamn tupperware! Instead, I suggest that you use the "Portion Size Method".

The Portion Size Method

Full disclosure, I did NOT invent the “Portion Size Method.” I first heard about it in Bill Phillip’s best selling book **“BODY FOR LIFE”.**

http://amzn.to/1XXAr2S

Then I came across it again in Dr OZ’s best seller **“YOU on a DIET”** (GREAT BOOK!)

http://amzn.to/21f1IzJ

A few years ago I came across my beloved "Portion Size Method" once again in Tim Ferriss' bestseller, "**The Four Hour Body**"

http://amzn.to/1dKZcny

Here are 3 diets that use the "Portion Size Method". When you see "protein, carb, vegetable, or fruit" it means to eat AT LEAST one portion of each. **A "portion" is the size of your OPEN HAND or CLOSED FIST.**

Sample Meal Plan For Someone Trying To Gain Muscle

7:00 a.m. Protein, Carb or Fruit
9:30 a.m. Protein, Carb or Fruit
12:30 a.m. Protein, Carb or Fruit
2:30 p.m. Protein, Carb or Fruit
5:30 p.m. Protein, Carb or Fruit
7:00 p.m. Protein, Carb or Fruit

Sample Meal Plan For Someone Trying To Lose Fat

If you're trying to lose fat, you should take out the carbs and only eat Protein, Vegetables. the great thing about this is that YOU CAN EAT AS MUCH AS YOU WANT AND STILL LOSE FAT because the eating only protein and vegetables will put you in a caloric deficit! (you should have some carbs ONLY after your workouts... more on that in the next chapter).

7:00 a.m. Protein, Vegetables
9:30 a.m. Protein, Vegetables
12:30 a.m. Protein, Vegetables
2:30 p.m. Protein, Vegetables
5:30 p.m. Protein, Carbohydrates or fruit (post workout)
7:00 p.m. Protein, Vegetables

Food Choices

Proteins
Fish
Chicken
Lean Steak
Lean Ham
Tuna
Salmon
Whole Eggs

Carbohydrates
Brown Rice
Wild Rice
Wheat Pasta
Oatmeal
Beans
Sweet Potatoes

Vegetables
Broccoli
Snow Peas
Peppers
Lettuce
Eggplant
String Beans
Spinach
Cucumbers

Fruits
Any fruit except fruit that has been canned.

In order to make the "portion size method" work, you HAVE to keep track of everything. Allow me to explain...

Keeping Track Of Everything

In order to make the portion size method work, you HAVE TO keep track of EVERYTHING!

- First you have to write down everything you eat EVERY DAY.
- Write down the TIME you eat everyday.
- Write down all of your workouts.
- You need to measure your waist line every week. (You have the option of measuring other body parts too, but you at least HAVE to measure your waist).
- Weigh yourself once a week.
- Check your progress every week and make changes to your diet and workouts accordingly.

By keeping track of EVERYTHING, you can easily see if you are making progress or not. But more importantly, you will know WHY you are making progress or not!

If you are not making progress, you can look at what you have been eating and make the changes to your diet and workouts accordingly.

The changes may be things like "eat less food next week", workout more frequently next week", "drink more water" etc... The key is to experiment every week until you find what makes YOU burn fat the fastest!

I go into more detail in this video--

http://bit.ly/1Q5s3eo

SECRET #2 Manage Your Insulin Levels To Maximise Fat Loss

"There is nothing either good or bad, but thinking makes it so."
— William Shakespeare

What Is Insulin?

It's human nature to label something as good or bad, but things are rarely that black and white.

People that want to lose fat think of insulin as 100% evil and think it makes us fat by inhibiting fat burning and promoting fat storage. On the other hand, those focusing on building muscle mass adore insulin because of anabolic and anticatabolic attributes.

The truth is, insulin is not "good" or "bad" as long as we know how to use it for our benefit.

Insulin is an anabolic hormone. In fact, it's even more anabolic than growth hormone. The problem is, it's indiscriminately anabolic and doesn't care whether it helps promote building muscle mass or the accumulation of fat. **It's main job is to maintain safe and steady blood glucose levels of around 80-100mg/dl.**

So when blood glucose levels rise above 100, insulin is secreted by the pancreas. Then, insulin takes the extra glucose out of the blood and takes it to a storage.

There are three different storage depots for extra glucose: muscle glycogen, liver glycogen, or fat cells (no good!). Of course we prefer storage in the former rather than the latter, but **insulin** does not give a shit. It simply regulates. Regulators. Mount up.

So let's look at exactly what insulin's job is--

Insulin's Good Side

1. Insulin Builds Muscle
Insulin stimulates protein synthesis by directing ribosomes to make more protein. Muscle is made of protein. Protein is manufactured by ribosomes. Ribosomes are turned on by insulin.

This means that insulin is required to build muscle!

2. Insulin Inhibits Catabolism of Protein
Insulin stops the breakdown of muscle. It may not seem as exciting, but the anti-catabolic nature of insulin is every bit as important as its anabolic nature. Whether or not you gain muscle mass over time is like a math game. *To build muscle, you must synthesize more protein than you catabolize.*

3. Insulin Transports Amino Acids into Muscle Cells
Insulin actively transports amino acids directly into the muscle cells. Branched-chained amino acids (BCAA's) are escorted into muscle cells by insulin, a very good thing if you want to build and maintain your muscle mass!

[There are a lot of weak blends for BCAA supplements on the market. I was sick and tired of not being able to find what I wanted and/or having to guess how much (i.e. proprietary blends) of the BCAA's I was actually getting. That's why I created my own (no guessing) blend of potent, not to mention great tasting BCAAS called "Revolt". Visit http://amzn.to/23fsUvg for more information.

4. Insulin Increases Activity of Glycogen Synthase
Insulin increases the activity of the enzymes (i.e. glycogen synthase) which stimulate glycogen formation. This is very important as it helps ensure the storage of glucose in muscle cells, thereby improving performance and recovery.

In layman's terms, muscle glycogen formation results in much fuller, denser-looking muscle.
Sounds great right? But insulin also has an ugly dark side.

Insulin's Bad Side

1. Insulin Inhibits Hormone-Sensitive Lipase
Insulin inhibits an enzyme called hormone-sensitive lipase, which is responsible for breaking down fat. That's obviously not good because if you can't break down stored fat (triglycerides) and turn it into a form that can be burned (free fatty acids), you're not going to get leaner.

2. Insulin Decreases Utilization of Fat
Insulin decreases utilization of fat for energy, and instead promotes the burning of carbohydrates for energy. To put that another way, *insulin "spares fat."*

Although that's not good for our body composition, it makes perfect sense when you recall that insulin's main function is to get rid of extra glucose in the blood. And insulin will accomplish this by both storing more carbs and burning more carbs.

3. Insulin Increases Fatty Acid Synthesis
Insulin increases fatty acid synthesis in the liver, which is step one in the process of gaining body fat. But this depends on the availability of excess carbs – an amount above what is immediately burned or stored as glycogen.

4. Insulin Promotes Glucose Transport into Fat Cells
Insulin promotes the transport of glucose across fat cell membranes and into the fat cells. What do you think is going to happen when a fat cell receives more glucose? It's going to GROW and MULTIPLY! Translation: You are going to be SO fat!

Using Insulin To Your Advantage

Insulin is simply an anabolic transport hormone that does it's job. *It doesn't care whether you gain fat or gain muscle*. All it cares about is keeping blood glucose in the normal range. When blood glucose rises above normal, insulin will be secreted and will work quickly to restore normal glucose levels.

It's not up to insulin to secrete itself at the right time. It's up to YOU to stimulate insulin release at the right time, and in the right amount if you're really good. And there's a way to do just that.

Want To Gain Muscle?

If your primary goal is to gain muscle, then you want higher levels of insulin throughout the day.

You especially want high insulin levels after training to take advantage of the fact that at that time, the muscle cell membrane is extra permeable to insulin and whatever it is carrying (i.e. glucose, BCAA).

Want Fat Loss?

If your goal is strictly fat loss, then you want lower levels of insulin throughout the day, on average.

At first thought, some people think that having low insulin levels all day every day is the way to lose fat. But that is not going to work. When you're training hard (see "SECRET # 5") ...you are going to be training hard (RIGHT!?), Then you are going to need a more intelligent strategy.

Even if you aren't concerned with gaining muscle mass, it's still important to initiate some insulin secretion post-workout. This will stop the training-induced catabolism as well as shuttle glucose and amino acids into the muscle cells. Otherwise you'll find yourself losing valuable muscle and therefore hampering the metabolic machinery that burns fat!

You don't want to look skinny-fat, do you? For some it would be a great alternative, but it's still nothing worth aspiring to. And skinny fat is exactly what you'll be unless you routinely give your muscles the needed carbs.

Want to Gain Muscle and Lose Fat?

Now here's a goal everyone can relate to: gaining muscle and losing fat at the same time.

Sadly, most of us believed others when they told us that it wasn't possible to gain lean muscle while losing body fat. Conventional wisdom still says that one must alternate between "bulking" and "cutting" cycles to achieve more muscle mass with less body fat. But this so-called wisdom isn't so wise after all.

You can not burn fat and build muscle at the EXACT SAME TIME, but you can do both in the same day! Let me explain.

When blood glucose is high, insulin is secreted and glucose is stored in muscle glycogen or liver glycogen. When blood glucose is low, insulin secretion is diminished and fat becomes the body's primary fuel source.

Insulin is like a switch that controls from moment to moment whether we're burning fat or building muscle. It doesn't take a whole day for this change to occur. In fact, it only takes minutes!

What this means is that you can plan your day to have periods of time focused on building muscle and periods of time focused on burning fat. And you can manipulate the length of these periods to alter the rate at which you gain muscle and lose fat.

Want to gain muscle faster? Increase the amount of insulin you secrete. This is especially beneficial to do immediately after resistance training for many reasons, one of which is because insulin will not convert glucose to fat if it can first store it as glycogen. And after an intense weight-training session, both muscle and liver glycogen are depleted and ready to soak up serious glucose. So, don't be shy with the carbs at this time.

For even faster muscle gain you should also boost insulin levels another time or two throughout the day. You could accomplish this with a couple more carb-containing meals. You could either have one of these prior to training and one after, or both after training (and after your post-workout drink).

Then, in order to cover the fat loss part of this equation, keep insulin levels low during the remainder of the day.

Flip the Switch
Whether you're promoting muscle gain or maximizing fat loss, insulin is the switch you need to learn to flip: "on" for muscle gains, "off" for fat loss.

Whichever you choose, remember that the switch doesn't have to stay flipped up or down for weeks or months at a time. Choose to manipulate insulin on a DAILY basis and you can reap the benefits while avoiding the drawbacks.

A great way to do this is with a method called "Carb Cycling"

Carb Cycling

Carb Cycling is a low/no-carbohydrate diet with intermittent periods of high or moderate carbohydrate consumption; essentially you are cycling your carbs to achieve a desired result. Most people have the misconception that consuming low carbs on a day to day basis for long periods of time is good for them. The main problem with low-carb diets is that they are meant as temporary diets; they deplete your energy and strength and are not the best method when attempting to lose body fat and retain muscle. You cannot eat that way forever. Your body needs carbs for daily functions.

This is where carb cycling comes in! With carb cycling you get the rapid fat loss of a low-carb diet and the ability to drop your bodyfat to a very low level without cannibalizing muscle mass and without the many other drawbacks associated with a low-carb diet. Carb cycling is an advanced technique requiring true dedication. I explain it more in the video below.

http://bit.ly/28FgsZS

Carb cycling is an eating plan with alternating high-carb and low-carb days. In order to lose weight, our bodies need the right combination of proteins, carbs, and healthy fats. Here's why:

Protein builds and maintains muscles and these muscles burn calories like an inferno. Protein also breaks down more slowly than carbs and fat, which burns even more calories and helps you feel fuller longer.

Carbs are the preferred fuel source for your muscles and organs, and they come in healthy versions (vegetables, fruits, grains, and legumes), and not-so-healthy versions (cakes, cookies, soda, doughnuts, candy, and many processed foods). Healthy carbs are also crucial for burning calories, and since they break down more slowly than those not-so-healthy carbs, they keep your blood sugar and energy levels steady, and they also keep your calorie-burning furnace hot so it burns more calories!

Healthy fats (unsaturated and non trans fats) consumed in moderation help the development and function of your eyes and brain and help prevent heart disease, stroke, depression, and arthritis. Healthy fats also help keep your energy levels steady and keep you from feeling hungry.

So why do we alternate high-carb and low-carb days in carb cycling? On high-carb days you're stocking your calorie-burning furnace so that on low-carb days your furnace burns fat, and lots of it! This pattern tricks your metabolism into burning a lot of calories, even on those low-carb days. It's an amazing and well-proven method.

This is how I use carb cycling to get RIPPED. I simply allow myself to eat carbs on days that I lift weights. I do NOT eat carbs on my rest days or days that I only do cardio.

HIGH CARB / WEIGHT LIFTING DAY

On my high carb / weight lifting days my diet looks like this (see "The Portions Size Method" for more details)

7:00 a.m. Protein, Carb, or Fruit
9:30 a.m Protein, Carb or Fruit
12:30 a.m. Protein, Carb or Fruit
2:30 p.m. Protein, Carb or Fruit
5:30 p.m. Protein, Carb or Fruit
7:00 p.m. Protein, Vegetables

On my LOW / CARB days I ONLY eat proteins and green vegetables

7:00 a.m. Protein, Vegetables
9:30 a.m. Protein, Vegetables
12:30 a.m. Protein, Vegetables
2:30 p.m. Protein, Vegetables
5:30 p.m. Protein, Vegetables
7:00 p.m. Protein, Vegetables

Food Choices

Proteins	Carbohydrates	Vegetables
Fish	Brown Rice	Broccoli
Chicken	Wild Rice	Snow Peas
Lean Steak	Wheat Pasta	Peppers
Lean Ham	Oatmeal	Lettuce
Tuna	Beans	Eggplant
Salmon	Sweet Potatoes	String Beans
Whole Eggs		Spinach
		Cucumbers

Fruits
Any fruit that is not canned is acceptable.

Obviously, you will be keeping track of EVERYTHING and will be monitoring your results. If you are not losing enough fat each week, then you are going to have to cut back on your carbs during training day. If you are losing too much muscle, you should bump up your carb intake on carb days.

The key is to look at your results every week, and compare them to your diet and training to see what's working and what is not. Then make any adjustments accordingly.

As you can see, things are getting more and more complex with each chapter. If you are REALLY ready to take it to the next level, keep reading...

SECRET #3: How To Lose 14 Pounds In 14 Days With "Intermittent Fasting"

"I count him braver who overcomes his desires than him who conquers his enemies; for the hardest victory is over self."
-Aristotle

What Is Intermittent Fasting

Intermittent fasting is one of the simplest and fastest ways to lose fat that I have ever come across. While you are fasting, your body turns into a fat burning furnace! Intermittent fasting is just like you would expect from the name. There are many other kinds of intermittent fasting, but I will focus on the kind that Martin Berkhan at http://www.leangains.com/ presents which is intra-day fasting - basically extending the night time sleeping fast a bit longer. Normal people fast for 8 hours during sleep and then eat throughout the other 16 hours. In the leangains intermittent fasting program, it's the other way around – you fast for 16 hours and only eat during the remaining 8 hours.

When I do Intermittent Fasting I only eat between the hours of 3pm and 11pm. Basicly I skip just "breakfast", eat a late lunch as my first meal of the day at 3pm, then I'm done eating by 11pm. But you can pick any 8 hour window that works for you.

The First Time I did "Leangains" Intermittent Fasting, I lost 14 pounds in 14 days! I explain it more in the video below--

http://bit.ly/1ZRKWSm

You might be thinking, "By skipping a meal, I simply eat less than normal so I will lose weight, right?"

Well, yes. However, there is more to it than that. If you cut out an entire meal, you are able to eat MORE food during your other meals and still be in a caloric deficit (which is an important factor for losing weight). But as you know from the last chapter, not all calories all created equal. The timing of meals can also influence how your body reacts (see chapter 2).

Why Intermittent Fasting?

Although we know that not all calories are created equal, caloric restriction plays a major role in weight loss. When you fast (either for 16 hours per day, or 24 hours every few days), you are also making it easier to restrict your caloric intake over the course of the week. This will give your body a chance to lose weight because you're eating less calories than you're used to..

It promotes stronger insulin sensitivity and increased growth hormone secretion, two keys for weight loss and muscle gaining, but intermittent fasting helps your body use insulin better. The Importance of this was already explained in the previous section.

AN IMPORTANT CAVEAT: Intermittent Fasting can be complex for people who have issues with blood sugar regulation, suffer from hypoglycemia, have diabetes, etc. If you fit into any of these categories I highly recommend you check with your doctor before trying this.

Can I build muscle and gain weight while intermittent fasting?

NO DOUBT!

In fact, I have been intermittent fasting for a few months...building muscle, while my body fat percentage is staying very low! I've measured my gains. People around me are even saying that I look more ripped! I still eat the same amount of food as before, but instead of eating all day long, I condense all of my calorie consumption into an eight hour window (usually 2-4 meals).

Here is what my intermittent fasting day looks like on a day that I lift weights:

2:00 p.m. Heavy strength training in a fasted state.
I only take three things before the workout 1.) A fat burning aid called "Tea Rexx," 2.) 10 grams of Revolt BCAA's and 3.) Rebellion pre-workout.
For more info on the supplements (https://www.brolaboratories.com/)
3:00 p.m. Protein, Carb or Fruit
6:00 p.m. Protein, Carb or Fruit
9:30 p.m. Protein, Vegetables
11:00 p.m. Protein, Vegetables

This is what my day looks like if I only do cardio or rest:

2:00 p.m. Cardio in a fasted state. Again, I only take Tea Rexx for energy, 10 grams of Revolt BCAA's, and Rebellion pre-workout before my training session.
For more info on the supplements (https://www.brolaboratories.com/)
3:00 p.m. Protein, Vegetables
6:00 p.m. Protein, Vegetables
9:30 p.m. Protein, Vegetables
11:00 p.m. Protein, Vegetables

Does intermittent fasting have different effects on men vs. women?

Yes, intermittent fasting does affect men and women differently.

This article on 'Mark's Daily Apple' breaks down the differences between men and women and how they are affected by intermittent fasting:

"One study, which I've cited before as evidence of a benefit to fasting, found that while if insulin sensitivity improved in male subjects, female subjects saw no such improvement. In fact, the glucose tolerance of fasting women actually worsened. Ouch.

Another study examined the effect of alternate day fasting on blood lipids. Women's HDL improved and their triglycerides remained stable; men's HDL remained stable and their triglycerides decreased. Favorable, albeit sex-specific results. Later, both obese men and women dropped body fat, body weight, blood pressure, total cholesterol, LDL cholesterol, and triglycerides on a fasting regimen. These people were obese, however, and perimenopausal women were excluded from the study, so the results may not apply to leaner people or women of reproductive age."

Basically, men and women will have different experiences with intermittent fasting; we're all unique snowflakes (yep, even you) and your body will be affected by intermittent fasting differently than the next person's.

My best advice? Give it a try (***tracking your results***). Experimentation goes a long way.

Tips and tricks about Fasting

- **Don't be a spaz.** Stop wondering: "Can I fast 15 hours instead of 16?" or "What if I eat an apple during my fasted period, will that ruin everything?" Relax. Your body is a finely tuned piece of machinery and learns to adapt. Not everything is as cut and dry as you think.
- **Stay busy.** If you are just sitting around thinking about how hungry you are, you'll be more likely to struggle with this. For that reason, I time my fasting periods for maximum efficiency and minimal discomfort:
- **Zero-calorie beverages are okay.** If you want to drink water, black coffee, or tea during your fasted period, that's okay. Remember, don't over think it - keep things simple! My favorite zero calorie beverage is Fighter Fuel.
- **Concerned about losing muscle mass?** Keep track of your strength training routines to see if you are getting stronger, and use BCAA's such as Revolt to prevent muscle breakdown during workouts.
- **Caffeine will decrease hunger during fast.** I take TEA REXX during my 16 hour fast. It really helps suppress my appetite and burn fat!!!
- **Everybody will react to intermittent fasting differently**. I can't tell you how your body will react. It's up to you to listen to your body and see how making these adjustments change it.
- **Don't expect miracles**. Yes, intermittent fasting can potentially help you lose weight, increase insulin sensitivity and increase growth hormone secretion (all good things), but it is only ONE factor in hundreds that will determine your body composition and overall health. Don't expect to drop to 8% body fat and get ripped just by skipping breakfast. You need to focus on building healthy habits, eating better foods, and getting stronger.

To sum it all up, intermittent fasting can potentially have some very positive benefits for somebody trying to lose weight or gain lean body mass or both.

Men and women will tend to have different results, just like each individual person will have different results. The ONLY way to find out is with self-experimentation.

SECRET #4 How To Trick Your body into Burning More Fat By Manipulating Your Body Temperature.

"It's lonely and cold on the top... lonely and cold."
-Judy Garland

I'm going to let you in on a little secret. Most humans think that getting hot and working up a sweat is what will help us burn the most fat. But recently, scientist have discovered that **the human body burns much more fat when it is cold.** When your body is cold, it has to burn a lot of fat and calories in order to stay at 98 degrees (98.6 °F or 37.0 °C). If you can get your body cold enough, it will burn more fat faster than exercise and diet can alone.

On a TEDTalk video in 2010, NASA scientist Ray Cronise discussed how to lose weight by exposing the body to cold temperatures. Ray went from 1.5 pounds of fat loss per week to 4.5 pounds of fat loss per week after simply adding cold to his weight loss regimen. Cold exposure helped him lose 30 pounds in only 6 weeks!

Check the video out here: http://bit.ly/23bR9dL

As is referenced in Ray's talk, Olympic swimmer Michael Phelps diet consists of approximately 12,000 calories per day (holy shit!). The only logical way he could burn this many calories is through swimming in very **cold water.** It should also be noted that many other elite athletes have begun to exercise at cold temperatures.

Here are some ways that you can add cold exposure in order to burn more fat faster.

- Drink a liter of ice cold water first thing in the morning. It's great for cleansing/hydration plus when you consume something cold (such as ice water), your body must temporarily increase the rate at which you burn calories in order to keep you warm and to warm the cold substance that you ingested.

- Take cold baths or showers. I started taking **ice baths** recently. Not only do they increase fat loss, but ice baths also naturally increase testosterone levels!!!! The first time I tried ice baths, I used a real bag of ice. Now I use reusable ice packs. They stay colder longer, and they are a lot more fiscally conservative.
- Workout in the cold. I really like to workout in the cold. It makes me work harder because I want to feel warm quickly. Here is an example:

http://bit.ly/1UzGfsc

SECRET #5: How To Burn More Fat By Working Out LESS

"Efficiency is doing things right; effectiveness is doing the right things."
-Peter Drucker

HIIT Cardio

What if I told you that you could burn more fat by doing less cardio? Well, with High Intensity Interval Training (also known as HIIT) you can do just that - burn more fat while spending less time in the gym. This is still a fairly new and cutting-edge type of cardiovascular training.

You have probably been told, just like the rest of us, that in order to burn the greatest amount of fat you need to do cardio for 20 to 60 minutes at a moderate intensity. This will indeed melt the fat away, but HIIT is a more efficient and athlete-friendly way to train and burn fat at the same time.

How HIIT Works:

With HIIT, you will be working harder than you normally work but for about a quarter to a half of the time that you would normally spend on the cardio machine of your choice.

Here's What You Do:

Perform a 5 minute warm-up. You can jog, do jumping jacks, whatever. Just get your body warmed up and ready to go.

Then take time to stretch properly and you are ready to begin.

Start at a moderate pace for 1 minute, then crank up the pace to 90 or 95% of your Maximum Heart Rate (MHR).

Continue at this effort for 15 to 20 seconds, then slow down to your starting pace for another minute followed by another all-out sprint for 15 to 20 seconds.

To achieve a similar result without running or using any machines you can pick a spot then jump as high as you can, as fast as you can over and over for 30 seconds followed by resting for 30 seconds. Repeat this for no more than 15 minutes.

Here is a video of me doing HIIT with a jump rope: http://bit.ly/1ZRKW4Y

If you perform this right I guarantee that you will be totally exhausted after 10-15 minutes.

Here is another video of me doing HIIT with a punching bag: http://bit.ly/1ZRL6JC

Benefits of HIIT

A study at Laval University in Quebec, Canada found that HIIT cardio helped trainees lose nine (yes, 9!) times more fat than those who trained the traditional way (moderate speed for 20-60 minutes). Combine HIIT with your weight program and you boost your metabolism through the roof!

If you want a comprehensive training system, you should check out my personal HIIT workout plan, Direct HIIT: http://www.directhiit.com/.

The Reason HIIT Is So Successful:

When you work at a high intensity, you burn more total calories per pound of body weight.
High intensity workouts such as weight training and HIIT boost growth hormone levels and elevate the body's metabolism throughout the entire day! What does this mean for you? The more calories that you burn in a day, the more weight you are able to lose. Even if weight loss is not your goal, HIIT is for you. Athletes will see better gains from doing HIIT cardio as opposed to traditional cardio.

Unless you are training for a marathon, you do not keep a constant pace during your sport. All sports whether it be soccer or football, even baseball or basketball have a point where you need to change gears and hit a full sprint.

HIIT will not only help your cardiovascular system, but will train the anaerobic ATP/CP system as well. Not only will you increase your cardiovascular endurance, but you'll improve your raw speed and explosiveness as well!

What Is ATP?

Otherwise known as adenosine triphosphate, ATP is critical to the release of energy. ATP is an adenosine-derived nucleotide that supplies large amounts of energy to cells for various biochemical processes, including muscle contraction and sugar metabolism, through its hydrolysis to ADP.

Here is another video of me explaining the benefits of HIIT-- http://bit.ly/1ZRL6JC

Resistance Training

First and foremost resistance training speeds up your metabolism of fat. Your body becomes more efficient at burning calories as a result. Picture two cars in a race. Car A is small in frame, but it has a huge engine. Car B is very large and heavy and has a very small engine. Which one do you think will go ten miles in the shortest amount of time? Your muscle mass is your engine, and the larger it is in proportion to your frame, the more efficient you become as a machine.

Balancing Your Body

When you build muscle mass, your muscles actually gobble up calories from your food in order to maintain themselves. This leaves fewer excess calories lying around, to turn into fat. In fact, if you lower your calorie intake just slightly, your new muscle mass will feast on some of your body fat.

Weight training increases your heart rate. Yes, it is an anaerobic exercise, not designed for fat-burning the way cardiovascular exercises are, but between sets your heart rate remains elevated. This allows you to get a bit of the aerobic effect throughout your workout especially if you don't rest for too long between sets. When I am in full-on fat burning mode, I only rest about 30 seconds between each set. This keeps my heart rate sky high for the whole workout! The best way to take advantage of this is to use a light to medium amount of weight and do a lot of repetitions (for example, 4 sets of 10-15 reps.)

I would like to give you a full resistance training program right now, but that is kind of beyond the scope of this 99 cent book. Here is great full body workout you can try-- http://bit.ly/263raXJ

I frequently post plenty of resistance training advice on my YouTube Channel.

SECRET #6: How To Burn Fat In Your Sleep

"My father said there were two kinds of people in the world: givers and takers. The takers may eat better, but the givers sleep better."
-Marlo Thomas

Every day people ask me about what supplements I take and what foods I eat to stay in shape. I'm surprised that nobody ever asks me, "How much do you sleep?" ...because **one of the easiest ways to burn fat and build muscle is to simply get more sleep**.

How Sleep Helps You Burn Fat

Research published this month in the Annals of Internal Medicine (one of the the big kahunas of peer reviewed medical journals) establishes that sleep - and sleep alone - is one of the most powerful diet tools ever identified:

http://bit.ly/1YrVHMp

There's not a diet pill on the planet that could accomplish what sleep did in this study, which compared two groups of overweight non-smokers on calorie restricted diets for 14 days. One group clocked 8.5 hours of sleep per night, and the other logged 5.5 hours of sleep per night (which the authors point out is a "norm" for people in this day and age.) Both groups ate roughly 1,450 calories a day. After two weeks, the people who slept more lost more fat than the group who slept less. More than half of the weight loss during the 8.5 hours of sleep was fat versus only one quarter of the weight loss during the 5.5 hours of sleep. People literally burned fat while they slept.

Even more startling, the folks who slept less lost more muscle (60% more muscle was lost by the sleep-deprived group). Those three hours of lost sleep caused a shift in metabolism that made the body want to preserve fat at the expense of muscle. And that's not all that happened: When the researchers compared circulating blood levels of appetite-regulating hormones in the two groups they found those who slept for three fewer hours had produced more of the appetite stimulating hormone ghrelin. As a result, they woke up hungrier!

Most of us assume our bodies burn more calories when we are awake longer, but that's not true. The metabolic rate is down-regulated with less sleep. Translation: When you sleep less, your body starts to burn calories at a slower rate to preserve energy. In the study, people burned on average 400 more calories by sleeping for 3 more hours - that's an additional 2,800 calories burned in just one week. With less sleep, the body seeks to meet the increased metabolic needs of longer waking hours by shifting into a lower gear, so to speak, that burns fewer calories and less fat.

Here is a video of me explaining the importance of sleep-- http://bit.ly/1XXFjVx

How Sleep Helps You Build Muscle

First, when you lift weights, what you're doing is actually tearing the muscle tissue in a healthy way. After you eat, your body uses certain nutrients to repair your muscle tissue. What you need to remember though, is that the protein in your body won't start repairing your muscle tissue until you are at rest for an extended period of time, such as sleep. What this means is that if you are lacking sleep, your body isn't getting sufficient time to repair and fully recover..

In addition to this, since sleep is the prime time for the body to recover from exercise, it's also when you will be rebuilding your torn muscle tissues. Without this recovery time, you're going to go into your next exercise session at a disadvantage.

Finally, you must not overlook the connection between the amount of sleep you get and your overall exercise performance. When you are short on sleep, it's quite typical to find yourself struggling to maintain a peak level of performance..

One of the key recommendations for combating over-training syndrome, which will quickly take you away from your workouts and limit further fat loss, is getting quality sleep. Failing to do so could mean you having to take time away from your program which, without a doubt, will slow you down.

So make sure you're getting 7-8 hours of sleep each night. Not only are you going to feel better, think clearer, and be much stronger when it comes to battling those food cravings that are so common with fat loss diets, but you'll also really be helping promote better long-term health as well. Like everything else, keep track of your sleep. Make note of what time you fall asleep and what time you wake. Did you get 7-8.5 hrs last night? If not, why? How can you make sure you get a successful night's sleep tonight? **Always remember, that which gets measured - gets managed.**

Bottom Line: If you want to burn fat, preserve muscle and wake up less hungry when you are dieting, sleep more…8.5 hours a night to be exact.

SECRET #7: How Eating Pizza, Burgers, and Fries Help You Burn FAT And Build Muscle

"Win if you can, lose if you must, but always cheat."
-Jesse Ventura

Cheaters DO WIN!

It's difficult to say to yourself "I will NEVER eat burgers, fries, pizza, cake, cookies or sweet ass drinks ever again". You're clearly bullshitting yourself if you think that's sustainable. The mere thought of that may keep you from even starting to eat right. That is why I recommend that one day a week you eat ANYTHING you want and forget about all of the DIET RULES I gave you for 24 hours!!! This is called a "CHEAT DAY".

I already know what you're thinking. "If I eat crazy for a whole day, won't I ruin all the progress that I made? No. ***You see, eating "bad" for one day a week will NOT hurt you, the same way that eating "good" one day a week will NOT help you! It's what you do consistently that counts***! <— (Tattoo that statement into your brain!)

Cheat days are not only fun, but they help you eat right the other 6 days of the week. It's easy to not eat a slice of pizza on a Tuesday if you know that you can eat 2 large pizza's and a 2 liter bottle of soda all by yourself on Sunday!

Plus, and even more importantly - cheat days actually HELP you burn fat!

How Cheat Days Help You Burn Fat

Anyone who's ever been on a diet can tell you that although things tend to start out well, that doesn't usually last long; after the first week or so, your rate of fat loss slows down dramatically. You might have lost 5-7 pounds in the first initial days, then you might only lose about half of that over the next several weeks.

Your hormones are to blame for this. There's a hormone called ***leptin*** that dramatically influences a number of mechanisms related to fat loss. Leptin is known as the "anti-starvation hormone". Leptin plays a huge role in controlling your rate of fat loss, because it controls a few other hormones that also affect metabolism and fat loss (most notably the thyroid hormones T3 and Tw).

Put in the most basic terms possible: when leptin levels are high, you can lose fat quickly; when leptin levels are low, fat loss slows down. The problem is that leptin levels drop when you're dieting!!!

Leptin levels are influenced by two things: the amount of body fat you have and the amount of calories that you consume. Your body fat percentage influences leptin because leptin is made in the fat cells; more fat equals more leptin.

Leptin's evolutionary function was to slow the metabolism and conserve energy (and fat) during times of famine. As a result, when you take in fewer calories, leptin levels decrease, helping you to survive the famine.

But if there is no famine, you are just dieting to burn fat. And when you're on that diet, you are decreasing fat mass and have a reduced caloric intake. As mentioned, this is a surefire way to tank leptin.

It basically works like this: lower calories -> lose fat -> reduce leptin -> stop losing fat.

This does not bode well for your fat loss efforts; the more fat you lose, the more difficult it will be to lose fat. This is why losing the last 5 pounds is in many ways harder than losing the first 50.

But here is the thing, if you increase leptin levels, you can start losing fat again!

And that is why you NEED to have a cheat day! **You see, cheat days aren't just about taking a "break" from dieting; they're a tool for helping you lose fat.** Remember, a big factor of leptin levels is your caloric intake, and a cheat day allows you to drastically increase the number of calories you consume, allowing for increased leptin levels.

Cheat days work! You should be doing it EVERY WEEK! It doesn't matter if you are trying to lose weight or gain muscle.

I am not the only one that is a strong believer in cheat days! “The Rock” talks about his weekly cheat days here-- http://bit.ly/1YrWnBy

Go crazy on your cheat days. Or you can just eat more of your favorite foods plus some treats you’d normally refrain from. But if you’re like me then you WANT to eat cake, pizza, burgers, and hot wings (my people LOVE *hot wings)!!!* I usually schedule my cheat day on Sunday, but it does not have to be the same day every week! You can change it to any day of the week when you have to go to a wedding, party, holiday, etc… Just make sure it’s only ONE cheat day per week...you cheater!

BONUS CHAPTER #1: How To Drink Away Fat

"Nothing is softer or more flexible than water, yet nothing can resist it."
-Lao Tzu

Drinking water is one of the simplest, yet most overlooked ways to burn fat and build muscle fast. Still though most people experience that they should drink "plenty" of water every day, few people follow it.

In fact, most people don't even experience how much "lots" is. If you want to gain muscle weight and/or burn fast, it's a priority for you to remain hydrated.

Water is vital for life, and only second in importance to oxygen. The human body cannot survive even a few days without water, while it can go for weeks without food.

Our bodies are 80 percent water, and our brains, 85 percent. But how will this assist you to gain muscle weight fast? Well, most (70 percent) of the lean muscle mass in your body is composed of water. So you need to drink a lot of water if you want to maximize the potential of your workouts and gain muscle weight fast; in fact, you need to drink a lot of it.

You lose water every day without you knowing it. For instance, sweating, you drop off 16 ounces of water, and you drop off another 16 ounces when you exhale throughout the day. You need other 48 ounces of water for the proper functioning of your intestines and kidneys.

So, just getting by requires 80 ounces or 10 cups of water. When you exercise intensely, your body's need for water goes up. If you're attempting to gain muscle weight fast, it's imperative that you ensure your body is always fully hydrated.

Studies show that a drop of 10 to 20 percent in muscle contraction can be caused by a mere drop of three to four percent in the body's water level. Keep in mind that building muscle is all about lifting as much weight as you can, for as many repetitions as possible.

To gain muscle weight fast, you have to drink a lot of water, especially before working out, to make sure that the 70 percent water content in your muscles is maintained.

When you're working out, water also prevents injuries. Extra stress is put on your connective tissues and joins when you train at high intensities over long periods of time. Water helps prevent injuries by cushioning and lubricating your joints. This will enable you to gain muscle weight fast, and will decrease the risk of injury in the procedure.

The digestive process also cannot work without water. The mainstay of any diet designed to gain muscle weight fast is protein. It cannot, however, be straightaway absorbed by the body's cells.

To allow the cells to use it to help you gain muscle weight fast, protein needs to be broken down into its component amino acids. To be able to do this, your body needs water.

Water also helps to regulate your body's temperature by keeping your skin moist through perspiration.

This becomes all the more important when you're attempting to gain muscle weight fast by performing intense exercise. Through urine, feces, sweat, and exhaled air, water also helps you remove unwanted waste products from the body.

So when you want to gain muscle weight fast and get ripped, it's paramount to ensure that you get enough water. Eight to ten glasses of water every day is what we've all been told to drink.
But when you want to burn fat and gain muscle weight fast, is this enough? I don't believe so at all!

You know you're drinking enough if your urine is clear. Your urine should be clear all the time (except 1st thing in the morning, and after you take your vitamins). If your piss is clear you're drinking enough, if your piss is yellow, you need to step up your water intake!!! I drink about 6-8 LITERS of water a day!!!

BONUS CHAPTER #2: 8 Ways To Naturally Increase Testosterone Levels

"You have to be a man before you can be a gentleman."
–John Wayne

Testosterone is a hormone that is secreted in both men and women. It is responsible for sex drive, as well as protein processing for muscle mass development and strength. The more Testosterone you have, the easier it will be for you to gain muscle and burn fat. Males produce about ten times the amount of testosterone as females do, but females are far more sensitive to its effects. Though testosterone is largely responsible for those traits and characteristics that are considered "masculine" – physical strength, body hair, dominance, and virility – both sexes require it for proper sexual and physical development.

Check out this video of me talking about increasing testosterone naturally-- http://bit.ly/1OqlpOd

1. EAT MORE FAT AND CHOLESTEROL

Our diet plays a huge role in our testosterone production. Our glands need certain minerals like zinc and magnesium to get testosterone production started and our body needs cholesterol to make testosterone.

To boost your testosterone levels you need to increase your fat and cholesterol intake. Studies have suggested that higher fat and cholesterol consumption results in increased levels of total T; men with low-fat diets typically have decreased T levels.

If you're anything like most people on planet earth you're currently thinking, "Isn't cholesterol bad for you?". The short answer is HELL NO!

Cholesterol is GOOD for you! Your body can not make testosterone without it! Your body NEEDS cholesterol to make testosterone!

If you're interested in learning more about the myths and benefits of cholesterol, I highly recommend reading this in-depth, well-written, and well-researched article:

"The Cholesterol Myth That Is Ruining Your Health" by Dr. Joseph Mercola
http://bit.ly/1GOwRxg

I eat at least four WHOLE eggs every night. It is important to do it at night because your body makes most of your testosterone while you are asleep.

Here is a video of me making EGG "MUFFINS"! You need to check this out!
http://bit.ly/1S5ReHZ

2. EAT MORE NUTS

Your testosterone levels will increase if you eat 20 Almonds at least 2 times a day. I can not find the clinical data online about almonds, but I did read in Tim Ferriss's book "The 4 Hour Body" that Almonds increase testosterone. Tim recommended eating 20 almonds 4 hours before sex for an extra boost! Because I live in world where I might have sex at any given moment, I am going to be eating 20 almonds at least 3 times a day. HERO MODE!

You will also want to add some brazil nuts. All nuts are little fat bombs that provide the cholesterol that cells need for T production. One study suggest that the selenium in Brazil nuts boosts testosterone. Try eating 3 Brazil Nuts 2-3 times a day.

3. TAKE VITAMIN D3

Vitamin D3 actually isn't a vitamin, it's a hormone - a really important hormone that provides a whole load of health benefits. Our bodies can naturally make vitamin D from the sun, but recent studies have shown that many westerners are vitamin D3 deficient because we're spending less and less time outdoors. When we do decide to venture outside, we slather our bodies with sunscreen, which prevents the sun reaching our skin to kick-off vitamin D3 production. If you're not getting enough sun, you may have a vitamin D3 deficiency, which may contribute to low T levels. If you think you need more vitamin D3, supplement it. Studies have shown that men who take this supplement see a boost in their testosterone levels. Because I have a darker complexion - which makes me prone to Vitamin D3 deficiency - I take 5,000 IU of vitamin D3 in the morning and 5,000 IU before bed for a total of 10,000 IU each day!

4. TAKE OMEGA-3 FISH OIL

Fish oil has been shown to improve heart and brain health as well as increase production of the Luteinizing hormone (the hormone responsible for triggering the testes to produce T). Because of the increased amounts of saturated fats and cholesterol you will be consuming, you want to make sure you get enough of the"good" fats to clear the gunk out of your blood.

5. LIFT WEIGHTS

If you want to increase testosterone, you've got to start lifting – and lifting heavy. Doing circuits with the weight machines won't cut it.

Here's what the research says on how to craft your weightlifting routine to maximize testosterone production:

Use compound lifts. Squats, bench press, deadlift, and shoulder press should be your main lifts. Exercises that work large muscle groups are associated with higher increases in testosterone.

http://1.usa.gov/1UdFmv8

Go for high volume. Workout volume is determined by the following formula: sets x reps x weight. Studies suggest that higher volume workouts result in higher T production.

http://1.usa.gov/1UdEJSh

Here is a good weight lifting workout you can try-- http://bit.ly/1Uk8Wft

6. DO HIIT CARDIO

You already know how much I LOVE HIIT!!!! So in addition to weightlifting, studies have shown that HIIT workouts can also help boost testosterone levels. For those of you who don't know, HIIT stands for high-intensity interval training. It calls for short, intense bursts of exercise, followed by a less-intense recovery period. You repeat with the intense/less-intense cycle several times throughout the workout. In addition to increasing T, HIIT has been shown to improve athletic conditioning and fat metabolism, as well as increase muscle strength.

If you would like to follow the HIIT training protocol that I personally use, check out Direct HIIT: http://www.directhiit.com/.

6. GET MORE AND BETTER SLEEP

Most Americans today are sleep deprived, which may be a contributing factor to declining testosterone levels in men. See, our body makes nearly all the testosterone it needs for the day while we're sleeping. That increased level of T that we experience at night is one of the reasons we wake up with "morning wood." (If you don't have morning wood on a consistent basis, you might have low T).

If you're not getting enough quality sleep, your body can't produce testosterone as efficiently or effectively. In one study, researchers at the University of Chicago found that young men who slept less than five hours a night for one week had lower testosterone levels than when they were fully rested. The drop was typically 10-15%.

Not only does sleep boost T, but it also helps manage cortisol, a stress hormone that has been shown to wreak havoc on testosterone levels when present in high amounts.

7. MANAGE STRESS

When we face stress, our adrenal glands secrete cortisol to prepare our bodies and minds to handle the stressful situation - the primal 'fight or flight' response. In small dosages, cortisol is fine and even useful, but elevated cortisol levels for prolonged periods can do some serious damage to our bodies and minds. One area that seems to take a hit when cortisol is high is our testosterone levels. Several studies have shown a link between cortisol and testosterone. When cortisol levels are high, testosterone levels are low; and when testosterone levels are high, cortisol levels are low.

Knowing about the connection between cortisol and testosterone, you should take the following measures to improve your stress management:

- Meditate for 20 minutes, twice per day.
- When you start to feel stressed, get up and go for a walk.
- Practice deep breathing exercises.

8. TAKE ICE BATHS

Take a 10-12 minute ice bath after hard workouts. One benefit I found in my research was that they could increase testosterone levels. I mentioned a 1993 study done by the Thrombosis Research Institute in England that found increased T levels after taking a cold shower. Sorry, I can not find the study online anymore, but ice baths were also mentioned in Tim Ferriss's book "The 4

Hour Body" as a great way to boost Testosterone and speed up recovery as well as aid in fat loss.

http://amzn.to/1RO1Eio

My good friend Dr. Farhan Khawaja has a GREAT video on how to naturally increase testosterone!

http://bit.ly/24RkBVG

BONUS CHAPTER # 3: Best Supplements To Burn Fat FAST

"If you don't have a competitive advantage, don't compete."
-Jack Welch

Not a day goes by without someone stopping me in the gym, on the train, or in the street and asking me, "What supplements do you take bro?" I secretly HATE that question because it implies that my physique is the result of pills as opposed to hard work and dedication. Having that said, there are a few supplements that I use to help me burn fat and build muscle. I have listed them below, but remember, they are not magic. They will help you reach your goals faster, but do not think that you can just take supplements and get in GREAT shape with minimal or no effort.

FAT BURNER

TEA REXX is the fat burner that I use everyday to stay ripped! A lot of other fat burning supplements make me feel like a crackhead because they have too much caffeine and unnatural ingredients. TEA REXX leaves out substances with dangerous side effects. What it does contain is 100% natural and mainly plant derived. It's even comes in vegetable capsules to avoid consumption of animal byproduct known as gelatin – which is what most other fat burners on the market use.

TEA REXX is safe and effective because it contains natural ingredients:

- Green Tea EGCG
- Green Coffee Bean extract
- Raspberry Ketones
- Ginseng
- Rhodiola Rosea
- Quercetin
- Synephrine
- Yohimbe
- L-Carnitine
- Yerba Mate
- Ginseng
- Rhodiola Rosea
- Moringa Leaf Powder

TEA REXX combines the most concentrated form of green tea extract available with raspberry ketones, green coffee bean, quercetin, L-carnitine, yohimbe, yerba mate, & more. This blend of super antioxidants, herbs, and amino acids gives you a tremendous amount of natural energy as well as fat burning capabilities.

TEA REXX is available HERE: http://amzn.to/1ipVTrr

BCAAs

REVOLT is another supplement I use daily to maintain my hard earned muscle mass. I, as well as millions of other fitness enthusiasts use BCAAs to prevent muscle catabolism. You have likely heard of the term BCAA thrown around in bodybuilding magazines and in supplement ads. Most people, though, have no idea what the term really means.

Muscle is made up of protein, and protein is made up of macromolecules called amino acids. BCAAs are basically the grouping of the amino acids **leucine, isoleucine**, and **valine**. These amino acids are essential because they are not produced naturally by the body and have to be acquired through food or supplementation.

Training on an empty stomach is a bodybuilding inside secret for acquiring maximum fat loss. Unfortunately, training in this manner also depletes you of energy as you are essentially pushing your body without fuel. Not only does this diminish performance but it could also catabolize your muscles.

REVOLT is a supplement designed to help maximize fat loss while preserving every ounce of hard earned muscle. Even if you don't train on an empty stomach, you can still lose muscle through other factors, such as doing too much cardio or consuming an unhealthy diet.

REVOLT is available HERE: http://amzn.to/23fsUvg

PRE-WORKOUT

Right before I perform heavy weight training or HIIT cardio, I use REBELLION pre-workout. Not only is REBELLION the best tasting pre-workout on the market, it is specifically formulated to increase your physical performance and intensity, amplify your muscle pump and endurance, and it helps carry you through amazing workouts.

The secret is a potent, time tested combination of ingredients including creatine, beta alanine, citrulline, betaine, caffeine, and black pepper extract. Each individual is a powerhouse. When combined into one high voltage pre-workout system, they give you the explosive energy, earth shaking power, relentless vigor, and the necessary endurance to help you finally build that rock solid super-hero body you desire.

You can find REBELLION Pre-Workout HERE: **http://amzn.to/1UVklKy**

COFFEE

If you guys have ever watched a day in the life video of mine or heard me talk about how I start my mornings you know I roll out of bed and go straight to the kitchen for coffee. This has been my routine for years. The problem was that I never really found a coffee that I loved. Some were good, but I wanted something better. That led me to create Fighter Fuel.

Fighter Fuel gives you a more powerful jolt without drastically increasing the caffeine. What most people don't know is that you get more caffeine from a light roast coffee as opposed to a medium or dark roast. Not only is Fighter Fuel a premium extra light roast coffee but it also contains panax ginseng which carries a host of additional vitality benefits.

Fighter Fuel will do more than just give you a slight "buzz" in energy; it will make you feel super charged and ready to train like a mutant on a mission. As mentioned, the energy rush comes from only two ingredients: **Caffeine from a premium extra light roast of 100% Arabica coffee and Panax Ginseng.**

You find out more about and order Fighter Fuel HERE: http://amzn.to/1OqKXff

BONUS CHAPTER #4: How To Motivate Yourself To Workout

"Somebody may beat me, but they are going to have to bleed to do it."
-Steve Prefontaine

Another question I get all the time is "How do you stay motivated to workout?" In the video below, I will explain how I stay motivated to workout and eat right every day. I think it will help you too:

http://bit.ly/1Pupahl

Here are some more tips to stay motivated:

1. MAKE EXERCISE PART OF YOUR DAILY ROUTINE

Exercise should be a regular part of your day, not something sporadic. Just as you set aside time for meals, sleep, School and/or work, set aside time for exercise. Pencil it in on your calendar, program it into your smartphone and stick to it just like you would any other important appointment. For best results, you may find that exercising at the same time and on the same days each week (such as first thing in the morning Monday, Wednesday, Friday and Saturday) helps you stay on track.

2. PICK A SPECIFIC GOAL

Goals that can't be measured can't be attained. You need to be able to determine whether you've reached your goals or not. For instance, a goal like "Get in better shape" is not easily measured, but a goal like "Have a 32 inch waist by July 4th," is. Don't start your resolutions until you have a measurable goal, or you will almost certainly fail.

3. MEASURE, MEASURE, MEASURE!

You must measure your progress, because when you see that you have progressed, you'll be motivated to keep going. If your goal is to lose weight, or gain muscle mass, I STRONGLY suggest that you stay off of the scale!!! Scales are grossly misleading! If you're trying to lose weight, you may be losing A LOT of FAT but you can end up weighing the same (or MORE) because you have gained muscle!

The same goes for people trying to gain muscle. The scale may tell you that you're not gaining, or that you're gaining really slow, but you're probably gaining a lot more muscle than you think. The weight may be staying the same because your workouts are burning your extra body fat off!

The best way to measure your progress is with a tape measure! I am going to go into more detail on this subject in upcoming blogs, but for now, just know that measuring inches you lose on your waist is the best way to tell if your losing fat or not. If you're trying to gain muscle mass, it's best to measure your arms, shoulders, chest and legs to see how much you have gained. I suggest you take your measurements once a week and make sure you keep records of your progress.

4. PLAN YOUR WORK AND WORK YOUR PLAN!

A goal without a plan is just another idea that will never come into fruition. You NEED to know the time you're going to workout everyday, and you need to know EXACTLY what you're going to do! If you're not following a detailed workout routine, it's highly likely you're just wasting your time!

You do NOT want to be one of those guys aimlessly wandering around the gym, not knowing what to do! Or even worse, you don't want to be in there talking to people like the gym is the happy hour spot! If you're going to do that, you should just stay home and pretend to work out there!

5. BE CONSISTENT

This is one of the most important tips! Here is a video:

http://bit.ly/1Q5E97A

Here is a video on how to MAKE time to workout everyday: http://bit.ly/21n6A1p

BONUS CHAPTER #5: Top 5 Ways To Get A Six Pack FAST

"I have one speed, I have one gear: Go!"
-Charlie Sheen

The number one question I get everyday is "How can I get a 6 pack fast?" Unfortunately there is no magic pill or supplement that will give you 6 pack overnight. But in the video below, I'll give you my top 5 tips that will help you get your six pack fast as possible:

http://bit.ly/1UVqCv9

1. GET YOUR DIET RIGHT

I am sure you all know that you're not going to get your 6 pack right by eating cookies and cakes everyday. You HAVE to have a solid nutritional plan. Without this you are just wasting your time. I wrote this book so that you have all the info you need to make this happen.

2. DO "HIIT" CARDIO

High-intensity interval training (HIIT) is an enhanced form of interval training, an exercise strategy alternating periods of short intense anaerobic exercise with less-intense recovery periods. When I Do HIIT cardio I normally only do it only 10-20 minutes. These short, intense workouts improve athletic ability and condition, increase metabolism, and burn fat WAY faster than traditional cardio. There are many ways to do HIIT. You can do HIIT by sprinting, jumping, jumping rope, and many other ways. I explain it further in the video below:

http://bit.ly/1ZRL6JC

3. TRAIN YOUR ABS WITH WEIGHTS

This is one thing that people always neglect is training abs with weights! I am always shocked when I find out that many people are not doing this (or doing it enough). If you are not training your abs with weight as least half of the time, I really think you are missing out! The video below explains this better:

http://bit.ly/1ZRVr8o

I recommend that you train your abs with weights every other time you train your abs. When you are not training your abs with weights you should be doing bodyweight only ab workouts. If you do not have a weight set, you can use a bookbag full of books. Here is a good ab workout using just bodyweight:

http://bit.ly/1UVpWG4

4. DO NOT TRAIN ABS EVERYDAY!!!!!!!

One thing that I hear a lot is "Hey Big Brandon, I workout my abs EVERY DAY but I am not seeing any results, what's up with that?" The reason people that train abs everyday do not see results, is because they train abs everyday!!! Like any other muscle group, you HAVE to give your abs a chance to rest. I think that training abs 2-4 times a week is fine. In fact I do not think that anybody should be working out everyday or you risk "Overtraining" and end up doing more harm than good. I explain it better in the video below.

http://bit.ly/1ZRXM35

5. BE CONSISTENT

This is by far the most important tip of all! If you are inconsistent with the 4 tips above, then you will see little progress. If you REALLY want to get a 6 pack, burn fat, or build muscle fast, then you have to be consistent!

Conclusion

"In the end, it's not the years in your life that count. It's the life in your years."
-Abraham Lincoln

Thanks for reading my book. I am positive that if you follow the advice written here, you will be well on your way to getting ripped faster than you ever thought possible.

I don't want to just sell you a book, I want to see the progress that you have made using everything you have read here.

Please keep me updated on your progress, send me before and after photos, and email me with any questions you may have!

Here are a few ways to contact me:

Fitness Blog http://www.BrandonCarter.com
YouTube http://www.youtube.com/HighLifeWorkout
Facebook https://www.facebook.com/BigBrandonCarter
Twitter https://twitter.com/BCarterMusic
Instagram http://instagram.com/bcartermusic
SnapChat: @KillerCarter187

20372460R00041

Printed in Great Britain
by Amazon